I'm Not That Woman

A Brand New Me & A Brand New Destiny

A Fatherless Daughter's Journey to Being

Angela Carr Patterson

Printed in the United States of America
Copyright © Angela Carr Patterson, 2012
All Rights Reserved

Published by:
Oasis Promotions Publishing
4611 Hardscrabble Road, Suite 193
Columbia, SC 29229

ISBN: 1475015593
ISBN-13:978-1475015591

DEDICATION

To the fatherless daughters of the world who never felt the safety and security of a loving dad, may the love you find within replace the love you've been seeking elsewhere. You can now rewrite your own love story.

To the women of The Love Story Women Circle and The Fatherless Daughters Network, may we continue this journey of celebration, transformation and love; and together we will raise the vibration of the planet.

CONTENTS

Angela Carr Patterson

ACKNOWLEDGMENTS

To Anita Fiouris who helped with the early work of this project and who would not stop until she made sure I finished this manuscript. You are the best!

To my parents, you have been my greatest inspiration and have believed in me, when I couldn't believe in myself. To my big brothers, Cliff and Robert, you have always been the wind beneath my wings. To my brother, Charles, I miss you much. Rest in peace. To my dearest Ashley, you know why I love you.

To my children: Tim (Tabitha), Brian, Crystal (Jarrod), LaVette (Rodney) and Courtney, you are my greatest motivation for being a better me. You make me proud to be your mom. To my granddaughters, Aubrie and Tori, you make Nana's heart leap every time she thinks of you.

To my husband Bill, thank you for creating a loving space for me to grow and expand. Thank you for simply standing with me as I live my dreams. I love you for being who you are, for loving me unconditionally and for being my divine right man!

Angela Carr Patterson

FOREWORD

"You know your profit is in your pain?"

"What do YOU want?"

"Don't DO – BE!"

At different times, stages and seasons, these tried-and-tested lightning bolt statements would jolt my entire body. I couldn't explain why after hearing those questions, billions of butterflies would flutter within my belly. I also couldn't explain why my spirit-man would come alive but my human-mind couldn't comprehend these conflicting concepts that, at times, were only translated in Greek, Japanese and Spanish. Now Momma didn't raise a slow leak. I mean I am quite proud to have done very well in my high school and college French classes. But my basic bilingual level of comprehension was way too elementary for a foreign language expert in matters of the heart: healing, loving and living fully.

As with any student, it would take many more "seed-planting" encounters with Angela before my series of personal "light-bulb" moments would set off like fireworks on the 4th at Disney World. And that's it exactly what my SERIES of personal, professional and spiritual revelations were like for me.

So as I read the pages of this great book, "I'm Not That Woman", my mind couldn't help but journey back to the beginning… our divine meeting place… It was at that place years ago that the Great Love Doctor began her subtle BUT life-transforming surgery on me. Interestingly enough, before I could come to the conclusion that I needed Angela in my life, in this capacity; I was already under "her anesthesia." Somewhere in the midst of me pushing and, sometimes, running away from the uncomfortable places her precious but power-packed questions would take me during brief follow-ups over the phone or email; IT happened! All I can remember afterwards was this motherly voice saying to me "…okay, all better now.

You'll need to drink plenty of water throughout the day and take it easy because we've done a lot of deep work." If you've had any type of surgery (whether it was in a hospital or dentist's office), you perhaps have experienced similar effects of coming to in a daze, scanning the room trying to remember where you are and why you're there.

What I know to be true, as I'm sure you will discover at the end of your reading (and if you're REALLY honest with yourself within the first couple of chapters), YOU deserve to take off the old man and put on the new! YOU deserve to forgive others and forgive you! YOU deserve to fall in love with you! YOU deserve and OWE it to yourself to take the time to read, reread and refer back to "I'm Not That Woman" for years to come.

As a former news anchor and television producer, now Media & Branding Strategist for 21st Century Femme-Preneurs, it is a MUST that I use my expertise in helping Angela broadcast her brilliance! Media producers, news stations, television hosts, reality shows and casting directors are always looking for fresh and exciting new content. They're also in need of industry experts that know their stuff, survived it and can passionately recreate the story for the masses to experience. We, perhaps, can all agree after reading "I'm Not That Woman" that Angela Carr-Patterson IS THAT WOMAN the world needs to see, hear, feel, learn from…and soak up every ounce of her timely wisdom and insight.

"I'm Not That Woman" is Angela's most amazingly transparent performance to date. As my personal Foreign Love Language Professor and Heart Surgeon you truly are doing "Life Work!"

Tia Brewer-Footman

YOUR Media Brand Strategist

I See You!

By Angela Carr Patterson

There comes a time in our lives when we must face the truth. We must face the truth of who we are; and the truth of who we are becoming. Our dance begins each morning when we awaken unto our day. We do this dance very well. We dance for our kids, we dance for our spouses, we dance for our bosses, and we dance for our parents and even the church. But when do we dance for ourselves?

We dance to entertain and please everyone around us; only to become invisible to ourselves. But I see you. I see you when you look into the mirror each morning to do your hair and your makeup while fighting the urge to break down and cry. I see you when you put lipstick on the same lips that so desperately want to shout to the world, "I am so tired...I am just so tired!" Not tired physically; you are tired and weary from the inside... within your deeper self.

I see you the moment you realize what is happening, when you regroup, square your shoulders, take a deep breath and grab your purse to walk out the door for work. You are on your way into the world to dance yet again. Oh, did I mention that before you left home you had gotten the kids ready, fixed breakfast, made some beds, loaded the dishwasher and folded a basket of laundry? You were dancing before anyone in your house had even woken up.

Now it's time to dance for your micro-managing, never-pleased boss and that noisy, jealous, aggravating co-worker who just won't shut up. I see you smiling while wanting to break down and cry. I see you working all day on a job that brings you no joy or gratification. I see you when your mouth curves into that grin while imagining owning that business you've always wanted. Then I also see you when you rationalize the moment away because you believe it is only wishful thinking. I see your grin disappear and your hope fade.

As you drive home, I see you plan your next dance of what to cook for dinner, how much homework you have to assist with and what time you have to go to Bible study. I see you when you grab your Bible for church and adjust your dance just a little because your swagger may be too much for the sisters in the choir. You don't want them to know that you have not had time to pray or read your Bible for four days. And you dare not act like you have any unanswered prayers. No, this dance that you have learned to do so well say to everyone, including the preacher, that all is well and everything is perfect because you love God!

But I see your pain, your hurt, your disappointments, your regrets and your unhappiness with your life. I see your desire for life to be more and I see your need for more. I see that you're stuck because you have bought into the false illusion that your life has to be this way. You have learned to dance the dance of making everyone a priority above yourself. Your illusion gives you permission to believe this is okay. Yet, I see your dance is getting weaker. I see you miss a few steps and turns only because you are getting older and you think it's too late to change the music or your dance.

My sister, I cry for you and I pray for you. Why? Because I know this dance all too well, and I also know it can be different. I am now dancing a new dance with new music and it is wonderful! I long to have all my sisters dance with me. I invite you to join me in this dance, and until you join me, I will dance for you ... because you have forgotten to dance for yourself

Introduction

As I sit to write this book, which I have been carrying around inside of me like a pregnant woman carries a child, I am reminded of the many reasons that I must share this message now. For years, I have attempted to share my story but I was either not ready, or it wasn't the right season, or I was simply afraid. Now, I believe with all of my heart that I am ready and the season is ripe. I wish that I could say that I am writing this book for all of the women who grew up without the love and assurance of a father. It would even sound nice and very humanitarian, but in reality; I am writing this book for Angela.

I write this book for me because I have learned that anytime I am genuine... I am also free. Yet, I know within my heart that many of you will close the last page of this book realizing that your life has been transformed because of it. My life has been transformed because I lived it. So yes, I share my story with you because of my love for you, and I share it because of my love for me. It takes courage to share parts of yourself that you have kept locked away inside the vaults of your heart. It takes courage to become transparent at the risk of appearing weak and even sometimes foolish. It also takes courage to risk being ridiculed and criticized for simply telling the truth. However, I am now ready to stand within my power and risk all of that for the hope that my story will touch someone.

My mother told me that my life began with trauma. I was a breech baby and had to be turned around with forceps before my mother could deliver me. Once I was born, my mother developed congestive heart failure. I like to say that I came here pushing my way through and knocking my mom's heart out in the process. I entered this world fighting to get here and my life has often felt like I had to fight in order to remain. I may have kicked my mom's heart out of whack, but I have spent most of my life trying to heal mine. I once read somewhere that babies remember the trauma they experienced during birth. I don't know if I remember mine, but I do know that most of my life's traumas had a lot to do with the heart...my heart to be exact. I simply wanted to be loved!

My story begins when William Daniel Carr met and married Annie Lee Taylor. Their story was one of a failed fairy tale. My mom had been married once before and from that union, my three brothers were born. Mom met my dad years later, dated for a while and then they actually broke up. She said one day out of the blue, he called and told her that he couldn't get her out of his mind and he loved her and wanted her. She dropped everything and they got married. Then some time later, I was conceived and they went their separate ways before I was born. They never reconciled the marriage.

I was told that my dad didn't come to see me until I was 3 months old. I don't remember seeing him until I was around 7 or 8 years old when my mother, in fact, took me to see him. I did not see my dad again until I was 19 years old. I was the one who went in search for him. I wanted to know why he never reached out to me and why he left me. I never got the answer to those questions.

It was not until approximately fifteen years ago that I came to realize how my father's absence in my life had shaped my foundational belief system. A belief system is the actual set of precepts that becomes the driven forces behind your thoughts, words and behaviors. My beliefs literally created insurmountable pain in my life. While my journey certainly has been filled with great pain, it also has been one of great triumphs, victories and joys. Every mistake made, every lesson learned, and every experience has helped me to grow in ways I can't even begin to imagine. Being a fatherless daughter has shown me that it matters little where you begin, but it's how you finish that counts.

Even in the midst of finally writing this book, yet another opportunity for a great lesson has arrived in my life. The man that I knew of as my father died. Just when I thought I had confronted all of my feelings about him, he goes and dies. My father's death caused things to surface within me that I didn't quite understand. In this book, I will share with you many lessons to help you live a better life, however, it is important for you to know that in the midst of writing this book I am also learning some very new lessons of my own.

This is not a very long book; in fact, it is a short read. I didn't feel the need to take too long to share what I wanted to say. But of course, we all know that big things do come in small packages. This work is filled with my truth as I know it; presented with honesty, love and a whole lot of transparency. This is not about blaming anyone for the challenges and pain in my life. When I share with you some of the things that were done to me and the wounds that were inflicted upon my life, please know that I don't mean to play the victim or to make anyone look defective or bad. I share these truths so that you can better understand where I was during that time in my life and how I was able to take one hundred percent responsibility for my life and move forward in triumph, in victory and in love. There will be some parts of this book where I will share what was done to me, but I may not share who did it. Please know this is done on purpose, not to protect the offender, but to keep the focus more on the healing process and the valuable life lessons; not the offender or the offense itself.

I have learned that my life has been as it should have been and everything that has happened in it was for a reason. I have also come to understand that many of the things that appeared in my life were a direct result of how I viewed myself based on my false belief systems. I am grateful for the lessons and what they've taught me. The most profound lesson of all is to finally realize that I am responsible for my own life and that anytime I don't like what is happening in it, I can choose to change it.

My intention that I hold for this book is to shine the light on the positive aspect of the "healing process" as well as on love, acceptance and forgiveness. I will share with you how my lack of self love and understanding for myself and others dictated the way I lived my life and how every negative circumstance led me to my "defining moments" that allowed me to choose to be different. A defining moment can come in many forms. It could be something that someone said to you, something you read, or simply a life-altering experience. Whatever it is, it will surely cause a paradigm shift and a radical transformation within you. You will see that my life continues to be filled with "defining moments" and continues to shift and transform regularly.

I love to use rituals in my life to help me download personal lessons and I will share with you some of my own personal rituals in this book. Every culture on earth use rituals to transfer information and encode behaviors that are deemed important. Personal rituals can help you build and shift into a better pattern for learning new ways of living and thinking. Through this book, you will come to know the power of rituals in your life.

Chapter One will serve as an informative look at what makes a fatherless daughter. We have been misled to believe that fatherless daughters are only females who grew up with an absent father, or else they are urban girls who grew up in poverty and in a home without a dad. I want to show you a different face of a fatherless daughter. In many cases, there is much to be said about a female whose father was there and the impact that his presence has had on her life to cause her to become a victim of the "fatherless daughter" syndrome. Many successful, highly profiled women, who grew up in a two-parent home with a great dad, still suffer from the fatherless daughter syndrome. You'll come to know the real meaning of a "fatherless daughter" and it's not what you have been led to believe.

I will continue with the following chapters in this book to share with you seven keys to unlocking a new way of being. I believe that it's not what we are doing that is keeping our lives stuck; it's who we are being. These seven keys are what I call, "My Journey to Being." These keys have been the driving forces behind unlocking the doors to who I have come to be …my complete, authentic self.

You won't find these keys written anywhere else because they originated from a deep place within my soul. That Distinctive Voice that can get into the marrow of your bones has downloaded these keys into my system and they are what I now use to live my life by. They have become the power base from which I source my life, run my business, and contribute to the world. These keys were the compasses I needed to find my way back home to love. They were the keys I needed to unlock the doors of my heart. They are the keys to me learning how to flow and live in the Love Zone. The Love Zone is the space where God and I exist as one, a space where I am my truest authentic, divine self. It is the space where I am complete, whole, perfect and loved. The Love Zone is where I am free to be who I was born to be.

I hope you will incorporate these keys into your life as well, maybe share them with a friend, a loved one, or even the world. I know that they work because I am a living example of this fact. I have left behind the broken pieces of a life I once knew and I can now say with a loud shout..."I'm Not That Woman!" I was a woman who was wounded, lost, and confused. I didn't know who I was, I didn't know how to love and I didn't know what to do about it. I discovered that I didn't need to do anything; I simply needed to become who I was born to be. I am doing just that. This is my journey and I pray it will become yours too, and together we will celebrate our new-found Journey to Being.

Angela Carr Patterson

1

The Making of a Fatherless Daughter

It has been said that the father-daughter relationship is the most important relationship within the family structure. I am no expert on the dynamics of the family structure and do not claim to be, but I do know that the impact of having an absent, unavailable or unattached father for a girl can have grave consequences on her life as she approaches adulthood. When this happens, it can and will affect the family dynamics as she begins to establish her own family unit. It will have an impact on her relationships with men, her career choices and even her relationship with money.

I define a fatherless daughter as a woman who grew up with an absent, unavailable or unattached father. The unavailable or unattached father could mean that he was absent due to divorce, death, or abandonment. The father could have been unavailable or unattached due to being a workaholic, alcohol or drug addict; or he simply lacked the ability to form a close emotional bond and could not demonstrate unconditional love. Whatever the reason, the life of that daughter will be impacted on many levels.

Every day, I speak to women from very diverse backgrounds, even from different parts of the world, who are now recognizing how their father-daughter relationship has had a dramatic impact upon them and shaped their lives on many different levels. Until most recently, there had not been a lot of discussions on the impact of the father-daughter relationship. Dads were considered heroes because they remained in the home with the mothers; they went off to work and kissed their daughters on the cheek or patted her on the head and told her how pretty she was. For the most part, it was acceptable that daddy be gone for long hours to work and provide for the family. Not only was it acceptable, it was necessary; and I understand that. It was normal for the father to leave the task of emotional bonding with their daughters to the moms. They didn't find it necessary to deeply communicate, spend enormous time or emotionally bond with their daughters as they did with their sons. Dads do not tend to view themselves as the primary caretakers of their daughters. And for the most part, they simply didn't know how. They bonded with their sons through playing ball, working in the yard, changing the oil in the car or watching the football game on television. As time progressed and we became adults, women did not see themselves as having issues with their fathers because this scenario was the norm in the family dynamic and structure. Women never expected to be closely bonded to dad as they were to mommy. The fact that daddy would give them a hug, kiss and say cute little things like "you're daddy's little princess" or daddy would give them money to buy that prom dress was usually enough, so we thought.

Then there is the world in which I grew up; in my world, there were no males in the home and this appeared normal as most of my friends didn't have fathers in their homes, either. It was rare that I visited a childhood friend whose dad lived in the home. I can remember on a few occasions when I would visit a friend who had a father in the home, I would feel very uncomfortable. The father's energy was unfamiliar to me; therefore, I felt unsafe. My life was surely that of a fatherless daughter. And those girls who didn't have a daddy in the home understood they were also fatherless daughters.

But where the danger lies is in the families where daddy was physically present, but emotionally absent, which would cause these women to be unable to identify their fatherless daughter's syndrome. The notion that fathers are not normally very close to their daughters explains why so many females described their father-daughter relationship as having been okay and that they didn't think they had any fatherless daughter's issues. But now that we are having this collective conversation, these women are now beginning to understand that it was not "normal" to have a distant, unattached or unavailable father.

I believe that no matter the reason for a father being unavailable and not forming a close, loving relationship with his daughter; the failure to do so, has predictable consequences on that daughter's life as she approaches womanhood. There are two distinct things that a girl must receive from her dad when growing up: unconditional love and security. When a father successfully demonstrates love for his daughter unconditionally; just for who she is, how she looks and what she does, he lays the foundation for her healthy self-image, self-love and self-perception. The second thing he must do is make her feel secure. She must feel that the world is safe and that those who love her are dependable, will protect her, and meet her needs. When this doesn't happen, trust becomes an issue for her throughout her life.

As adults, we fatherless daughters begin to judge our success in life based on the money we earn and the love we experience in our relationships. If we struggle or have challenges in either of these areas, we begin to feel unwanted, unsafe, insecure, and rejected. Thus, begins the making of a fatherless daughter.

In my Fatherless Daughter's Breakthrough Coaching Program, I created four Fatherless Daughter Archetypes that I believe most of us fit into. The four archetypes are:

· The **_Enchanted Daughter_** is addicted to love and craves intimate relationships. She is not happy unless she is in a relationship, but the relationship has to be "perfect". She fantasizes about her Prince Charming coming to sweep her off her feet and take care of her. She desires to be in love, but she is really addicted to her idea of love. She demands that her mate be perfect; and if he forgets to do just one small thing, she feels hurt or mistreated. It doesn't matter what is done for her; it's never enough and she is always the victim. Her beloved can do ten things correctly but make one mistake and she will focus only on the one mistake. Her mate begins to feel that she is just too hard to please and love. Yet, her greatest need is love, but her greatest fear is abandonment and intimacy. She has a controlling belief that, "If I hold onto you, I will be safe." And her daddy wound is: "I want my daddy to love me and take care of me."

· The **Solitary Daughter** finds it difficult to connect with people on deeper levels, and this has been the source of her pain. She is defensive and tends to guard her heart in the relationship with her mate and even with her own children, sometimes. People sense a distance from her because she appears to isolate herself, she will not let anyone inside and she is afraid to be open. She does not show up fully in relating to herself or to others. Her greatest need is connection, but her greatest fear is rejection. She holds a belief that says, "I will be hurt if I get too close." Her daddy wound is: "I am invisible and do not exist in my daddy's eyes."

· The **Superwoman Daughter** is driven, independent, and an over achiever. She is always striving to get to the next level in her career and her strong urge to be perfect can never be satisfied. Her identity is grounded in her external success; such as the money she earns and her personal achievements, instead of valuing who she is internally. She has a "take charge" attitude and can sometimes appear controlling and overbearing, which has cost her much pain in most of her relationships. Her greatest need is acceptance; her greatest fear is a loss of freedom and being controlled. She holds a belief that says, "If I am perfect and in control, I will be safe and they won't leave me". Her daddy wounds: "I want my daddy to protect me, accept me, and validate me".

· The **Pretty Woman Daughter** is constantly seeking closeness with a man even if she has to sacrifice herself for it because she has not recognized how to love the deeper parts of herself. She can sometimes be seen as promiscuous because often times she has traded sex for her need of real intimacy and closeness. Her greatest need is being valued and her greatest fear is disapproval. She holds a belief that says,

"I'll be loved and valued if I meet your needs." Her daddy wounds: "I want my daddy to value and approve of me".

I share these four women with you because on some level I have found myself in all four of them and know you can find yourself in them as well. Taking one hundred percent responsibility and seeing myself as the source of these patterns was an eye-opener for me and has been for many of my coaching clients. Getting clear about our underlying beliefs and assumptions about ourselves, about others and about life, and identifying the ways in which we have been showing up and responding inside of those beliefs is the first step to helping us to move our lives forward. Once we have identified these false, limiting beliefs, we can change them by deconstructing them through a new and more self-serving belief.

Your false belief may have served you well as a little girl, but now that you are a grown woman, this belief is no longer true for you. Until now, the little girl within you has been interpreting and responding to that false belief and giving it meaning. You can now choose a new belief and give it new meaning from your adult self. Constructing a new belief replaces the old beliefs and creates a new space for you to source your life and power from.

Summary:

Take a few moments to review each Fatherless Daughter Archetype to see if you can identify some of the beliefs that you may be carrying around with you. Or if you prefer, you can access our online Fatherless Daughter Archetype Assessment Tool at www.fatherlessdaughters.net . Whatever option you choose to select, I want to make sure that you become aware of what's driving your life's choices. Awareness is the first thing we can do to identify and understand our authentic self. Awareness will open the gates that lead to a more love-filled life.

Secondly, I want you to practice deconstructing that old belief by replacing it with a new one. **Example**: *Old belief—"If I get too close they will leave me and no longer love me." New belief—"I am safe and I am loved by all of life. I have the power to create deep, rich and meaningful relationships."* Read your new belief statements aloud at least twenty times each day for seven days. As you begin to do this, life will begin showing up in ways that are consistent with the deeper truth of who you are now becoming. This is the start of your journey to being.

In upcoming chapters, I will offer you my seven keys to helping you walk through the gates to a marvelous and brand new life.

2
Remembering Who You Are

It was a beautiful autumn day and I woke up feeling like someone had just cut my head open and poured all the blood out of my body. I felt depleted, weak, exhausted and just plain old miserable. I had reached a breaking point. I was depressed and was at a place where I didn't know if I could move forward. My marriage was failing, stress had made my body sick, and I was emotionally empty. So I pulled myself out of bed and I put on a pair of shorts, and a T-shirt. I didn't comb my hair, nor did I brush my teeth; I was barefoot and I didn't wear a bra...which by the way, was not a pretty sight after giving birth to three children. I jumped in my car, turned the ignition, and drove around the block to my best friend's house. I went to her back door, because I looked so bad, and I knocked loudly and rapidly. When she answered the door, she appeared startled; as if she had just seen a ghost. I guess I was looking pretty awful and most people that knew me knew that I would never leave my house looking that way. So immediately she realized something was very wrong. She reached for my hand, without saying a word, and walked me into her family room where she gently sat me down in a chair. She then knelt down in front of me with her hands placed on my knees and looked me square in my eyes. She firmly said to me, "I don't know where you are right now, but what I do know is that where you are, you cannot stay". Then she grabbed my hand and asked me, "What do you want?"

This was a defining moment for me, because up until then, no one had ever asked me, "What do you want?" Also up until then I had never made a single decision in my life based solely on what I wanted. It was always, "What did God want from me, what did my mother want, what did my husband want, what did my children want, or what was the best thing for everyone?" I never really even thought what I wanted mattered to anyone. I sat there for what I know was at least five minutes, struggling with what I now know to be the most important question of my life. I finally blurted out to her, "I want out!" I wanted out of a marriage that was killing me emotionally and physically, and if I didn't get out, I was going to die from the pain and the deep sadness. As the words, "I want out!" rolled from my lips, I felt a sense of liberation. For the first time in my life, I had said exactly what I wanted. I didn't consider what my mother wanted, what my children wanted, or even what my friends wanted. I made a decision based solely upon what I wanted; and it felt great!

It was also in that moment that I realized I hadn't known what I wanted because I didn't know who I was. I would soon begin a journey to answering one of the most important questions every woman must answer in order to move her life forward. "Who am I?" In order to move from where I was to a place where my life would change, I needed to discover "My real self." Before we can truly know what we want from life, we must know who we really are. That morning in Pam's house changed the course of my life forever. This was my invitation to discovering one of the most beautiful things on the planet. "Me"! It was my moment. My journey to self-discovery had begun, and little did I know it would be fraught with so many valuable lessons along the way. It became a journey that I had to take because it was the path for me to become everything I was meant to be.

The first stop on my journey was recognizing that who I had become was not even close to who I was born to be. It occurred to me that to change my life for the better, I had to stop projecting my false self all over the place. Many women view themselves inaccurately because of the unchallenged distorted beliefs embedded in their subconscious minds. We hold a self-image buried deep in our subconscious mind; and that self-image controls everything. It controls how you think, what you say, and the actions and choices you make. Your behavior will always be consistent with who you think you are. This is exactly what was happening to me in my life. There had been a gap between who I really was versus how I had been showing up in my life. I had before me the fearful task of peeling back the layers of my false self in order to discover the true core of who I was.

I had worked so hard to become who I thought others wanted me to be. I believed that if I placed my focus on the other person and not myself, and if I could live up to being what they wanted me to be, then they would love me and never leave me. Yet, that simply was not true and many people in my life confirmed this false belief by leaving anyway. The reason they left was because when I did show up, I was not my real, truest self. When we show up as someone else, not being authentic, it releases an energy from us as being distant and disconnected. As a result people see us as unapproachable, and even, unlovable. When others try to reach out to us, they get a feeling or sense there is no one there…you appear invisible. And really there isn't anyone there, because the real you is hiding somewhere in your fears. Therefore when people begin to back away from you, you start to feel rejected and unwanted. As I came to understand this, I knew that if I was going to experience any kind of true meaningful relationship with anyone, I needed the real "me" to show up.

So the question, "Who am I?" began to ring loudly in my ears. I just kept asking myself, "Who are you?" Then one day, a thought came to me that if I wanted to learn who I was, perhaps I needed to retrace my roots from the beginning. My first thought was to look to my parents. They were the ones who gave me life. But I realized they could not be the ones to answer this identity question for me, because much of my misplaced identity was a result of what I learned from them. Let me explain why I say this. Eighty percent of our emotional programming is implanted in each of us by the time we are eight years of age. That means that eighty percent of my identity, self-perception, thoughts, and beliefs were already in place before I was ten years of age.

With my mother being a single parent, she had to rely on my older brothers and grandmother to take care of me while she worked. I was the youngest of four children, with three older brothers who were ten or more years older than me. I can remember feeling like I never really had a place in my home. My brothers were normally out with friends or at work, mom was always working, and my grandmother was always raising hell, cussing me out, and beating my butt. As I became an adult, I realized that my grandmother was a very troubled and disturbed woman. She took her rage, anger, and sickness out on me daily. I grew up being called all kinds of names, such as bitch, ugly and heifer. This was the norm for me. When mom did come home, she was either tired or ready to go out with her friends. I learned early on to not tell my mom about my grandmother because then, my mom would face the wrath of my grandmother and she needed grandma to watch me while she worked. I also didn't want to tell my mom because she had breast cancer when I was five years old. I was always told that she didn't need to get upset about anything or the cancer would return. In my mind, I had to be the best, perfect daughter a mother could have. I had to be perfect and never cause her any worry or stress. I didn't want to be the reason my mom died of cancer.

Because of this belief, I learned how to keep a secret when someone did something to me. When a male family member would push me down on the bed and cover my face with a pillow, get on top of me and pleasure himself, I didn't tell that. When grandma would call me names or beat me mercifully, I didn't tell that either. When the kids at school would call me names and pick at me, I simply did not tell. My beliefs were now being formed. My beliefs were translated to me as "Protect your mother, don't cause any problems, don't make any waves, and be perfect". I felt if I could do that, I would always have a mom. I couldn't lose her…then what would happen? I already didn't have a dad. These beliefs became the mirror from which I viewed myself. This is how I identified myself. I needed to be perfect, I needed to be invisible and I needed to be quiet. I became the "Solitary Daughter."

Fast forward my life, years later, to my being a married woman for almost sixteen years with three children. Married to man who gave me sexually transmitted diseases, a man who had numerous sexual affairs, a man who mentally and emotionally abused me, a man who was a minister…a man who didn't pay his bills; and I couldn't tell anyone. So here I was at a place of deep despair and my friend had the nerve to ask me…"What do you want?" I finally said I wanted out. Yes, I wanted out!! I wanted out of that marriage, and I wanted out of the prison I built around my mind and my heart. I wanted FREEDOM in every sense of the word. Everyone around me was trying to tell me that I needed to stay in my marriage and that God would work it out. I thought to myself, God had 16 years to work it out, now I'm going to work it out myself. Little did I know, God was with me all of the way directing my every step.

We live our lives so carefully trying to emulate what we think others want us to be until we truly lose sight of who we were meant to be. And in my attempt to make sense of everything, to find myself, I finally realized that instead of looking to my mother and my father to truly discover who I really was, I needed to retrace my life beyond my mother's womb. I needed to direct my attention to my Source. To God who created me. God knew the answer to the "Who am I?" In the Bible, the book of Jeremiah 1:5, says, "I knew you before you were formed in your mother's womb". This scripture tells me that before I was my mother's child, before I was my father's daughter, I was God's creation. If I was to know my true identity, I needed to find it through God because my pain would never heal until I healed my misplaced sense of identity… because my life was responding to who I was being, not to who I really was.

I was already a Christian so I knew the basic practical teaching of the Bible. In addition, I also knew there was more that I hadn't yet discovered. I began to read everything I could about being made in the image of God. But what I would soon discover changed my life forever. Up until that moment, I had viewed God as being somewhere out there in Heaven and I was here on earth. We, Christians, are taught at an early age, "Our Father, Who Art in Heaven". So my emotional programming said to me that I was disconnected from God and if I wanted God to love me, I had to be, you guessed it, perfect and without blemish. In my attempt to do everything perfectly, to try and be perfect, I was left in total despair and defeat.

Believing that we are separated from God is the root of every problem we have in life. This belief will keep us struggling in pain and keep us defeated. We must identify with something much greater than ourselves; and for me that became my oneness with God, my union with The Divine. No one ever told me that I was one with God. It was as if a light bulb went off inside me. You mean God and me are connected? I didn't have to earn this connection, but the mere fact that I existed made me one with God? Wow! In that moment, I knew that my life had changed. God never ask to have a relationship with us, God wants oneness with us.

In the presence of God there is nothing but love. That's why I call it the Love Zone. It's where God sees me as perfect, loved, and lovable. It's that non-physical, divine part of us that is who we really are authentically at the core. Even more remarkably, we are all unique. The only people who don't know this are you and I because we have forgotten. Any time we act out in ways that are not in alignment with our oneness with God, it is because we are out of alignment with our divine nature and have forgotten who we really are. That's why deep inside of each of us, we can even feel it in our bodies when we do something that is not in alignment with who we are. Think about it. When you say or do something that is hurtful to someone, you feel it yourself. Why? Because that action was not in alignment with whom you really are and you are now in discord with your truest self. But all you and I have to do at any moment is remember who we are and get back into the Love Zone; live from that power base, allow our lives to be fueled from that space, and become who we really are once again.

My level of awareness to who I was and who I could become was now clearer. I was a part of a remarkable, invisible story that was unfolding and I could somehow begin to sense the greatness that was anchored deeply within me. We can become confused about who we are when we begin to see ourselves like everyone else. For example, the caterpillar knew he was born to be more than a crawler on the ground. He could have mistaken himself for a worm, because he was crawling around on the dirt with them. Also, people would tell him that he was a worm. People would walk by and say "Oh, look at that worm". Just because the caterpillar, like the worm, is crawling in the dirt doesn't make him a worm. The caterpillar is not a worm. Worms don't have legs, and the caterpillar does. We may become confused about who we are because people have tried to treat us less than we are. And more importantly, we have treated ourselves less than we are. We have thought that we were worms because we forgot to look closer to see that we had legs. Those legs are there to remind us to stand tall and embrace the truth of who we really are.

As we look closer within ourselves, to go deeper within, we will begin to realize that we have been fashioned and made in God's image and imprinted with His love. I love the ocean. It is both soothing and powerful. I love to look at the waves as they move so easily. There is such a seamless flow between the wave and the ocean that you cannot tell where one begins and the other one ends. So it is with us and God. God is the ocean and we are the waves...the same Divine power that exists in God, exists within us. The same substance that makes up the ocean also makes up the wave. The same love that exists in God exists in us. Wow...I am part of the Divine. No one ever really explained it to me that way. As I said before, I was always taught to believe that God was over here and I was over there. And if I messed up or did something wrong, I would be farther away from God. But how can I and God be one and then when I mess up, I am no longer one with Him?

What I learned is that when I do make a mistake, I make the mistake because I forget who I am. All I simply need to do is remember who I am again. This was an awakening for me and a real defining moment. This was a beautiful inescapable truth for my life. We are whole when we remember our oneness with God and outside of that connection; we become dissociated from our own essence. When we don't recognize our divine heritage, it translates into confusion about ourselves. We then lack our spiritual identity.

It is our job and our responsibility to go back to the Source if we want to remember who we are. I am a divine child of God, and that alone makes you and me more than enough. Now when I look at the girl in the mirror, well, I just blink and smile.

Summary:

The first step to *"My Journey to Being"* is: Remember Who You Are.

My Defining Moment:

When I was willing to let go of who I was not, step into my most powerful space and become who I was born to be.

Steps to Remembering Who You Are:

1. Retrace your life beyond your mother's womb, by understanding who God says you are.

2. Allow your spiritual identity to be the power base from which you now live your life.

3. Believe that you and God are one.

My Ritual:

For thirty days I wrote a brief description of who I was without giving any reference to my work, my children, my husband or my parents. Ask yourself this question: who am I at the core? Be very descriptive. Don't try to control the thoughts, just let them flow and write until you can't write any more. Each day, your self-image will become more and more clear. You will start to hear God as He whispers to you, who you are.

_____

_____

_____

_____

_____

_____

3

Reunify to Love

I can remember going to church as a young girl and hearing the preacher say that God was my father. That didn't sit too well with me because my father was nowhere to be found. I didn't see him and did not I hear from him at all. I also never saw God or heard from him. Therefore telling me that God was my father was not such a good idea.

I did, however, always pray and ask God for help. Somehow, not seeing Him didn't ever stop me from trying to talk to Him. As a young girl, I would find myself bargaining with God. I would say things like, "God if you send me a daddy, I will be a good girl." I wanted my daddy so badly, but I was very careful not to let anyone know. It was my secret. I thought if I complained to my mother, it would upset her and the cancer would return. It's amazing how young minds think and how, as children, we are so quick to take on blame.

My mother was a single parent who worked a lot and worked some long hours. My primary caretaker was my grandmother who, in my opinion then, was the meanest woman on the planet. My grandmother was a mixture of Tyler Perry's fictional character, Madea, and the mean character, Mary Jones, from the movie, "Precious". My grandmother could curse you out and call you some of the most awful names. I would be so confused because one moment she was calling me "baby" and in the next split second I was a bitch or heifer. I don't ever remember once my grandmother telling me that she loved me. So here I was; no daddy, mama always gone, and grandma cursing me.

In midst of all the daily chaos, I just wanted someone to love me. I can remember going the bathroom and crying out to God to please rescue me. A girl learns to love herself through the love she sees reflected back to her in her father's eyes. If her dad was not around or even if he was there and did not show her unconditional love for who she is, the very existence of that girl will not have been validated. She will then spend her entire life seeking love and validation in all the wrong places.

As a fatherless daughter, I was trying to find love in my home; and on many levels, what I really experienced was pain. I would try so hard to earn a little love from my grandmother by being really quiet, not asking for anything and being very good. It didn't take much to set her off and send her into a rage; and often times I was on the butt end of that rage mentally and physically. But who was I going to tell? Remember, I couldn't tell my mother because I didn't want her stressed or upset.

Then one day, as if it couldn't get any worse, my niece and nephew came to live with us when I was nine years old. They were younger than me, but my life went into a tailspin once they arrived. All the attention and focus went to them. Not that I was getting a lot of attention before they arrived. I can remember me wanting my mother's attention and her saying to me, "You know I love you, I've got to show them that I love them." I wanted to say, "How do I know that you love me?" I felt like I was invisible. After my niece and nephew arrived, my mother began to be home more, but it was not to spend time with me, but with them. There were times she would take them out with her and leave me home with the green eyed monster...my grandmother. It was during those times that I really began to think that something was wrong with me. I believed that I was not lovable and could never be.

I believed that I alone wasn't enough and I needed to be perfect for anyone to love me. My father didn't want me, my grandmother didn't like me and my mother avoided me. As children, we don't have the ability to filter what happens to us through logic and understanding. We filter everything through our emotional feelings. Therefore, my interpretation as a young girl was "I'm not wanted or needed." Now that I am an evolved adult, I realize the enormous responsibility that my mother carried with raising her own four children, two grand-children and caring for her mother...plus running a hair salon. My mother single-handedly did all of this without a husband. I now understand why she didn't have a lot of time for anyone. But before this realization came to be, my life was being driven by an unconscious belief that I was invisible and unlovable.

When I was thirteen years of age, my mother married my step dad; who I might add, is who I call my real father. I can remember feeling so very happy because now I had a dad. My mom was happy and the story would have a happy ending...right? No! My step dad was in the military, and about nine months after they were married he was sent off to a new duty station, located in California. We remained behind in South Carolina. Can you believe this!! I finally get a dad and then he's gone. I was so upset and didn't understand why we couldn't go with him.

But before he left, my mother spent an enormous amount of time bonding my step dad with her two new younger children...my niece and nephew. I was now a teenager and, in my mind, I didn't seem to fit into their little blended family. I am sure it was difficult to bond a teenage girl with a new husband, but I felt even more invisible. All I wanted was to be noticed and to be loved. I spent the next few years feeling isolated and not believing that I fit anywhere. Let's fast forward to my senior year in high school when I met him. He was handsome, fine and he wanted me. So I married my husband when I was 17 years old.

I wanted to follow love. At least I thought it was love. I would soon discover that the marriage was filled with anything but love. How could I have known? I didn't know what love looked like. We all can remember when we learned to ride a bike, we know who taught us how to drive a car, but do you remember who taught you how to love? Do you remember anyone sitting you down and saying, "This is how you love" or "This is what love looks like"? No, we learn how to love through the people who modeled it in front of us. My love lessons were truly screwed up. These are the lessons that I learned: I learned that people who love you also hurt you. My grandmother was a wounded soul who took her pain out on me every day. I would have done anything to make my grandmother love me. She just didn't know how to love. She was filled with rage and anger and I was her release. Then I was sexually abused by someone who was supposed to care about me. My biological father, who was supposed to love me, abandoned me. My ex-husband was supposed to love me but he slept around on me. So my love lessons shouted very loudly to me, "People who love you, also hurt you."

Yet, I still yearned and craved for someone to love me. After my divorce, I felt lonely and desperate. I needed and wanted someone to just hold me. There were times when I ended up in the arms and beds of men who only wanted my body. Often times, I was willing to give them my body if they would just pretend to love me. I was like an addict who needed a fix. My fix wasn't sex, I just wanted closeness. I wanted to be connected. I can remember feeling so excited and like I was on some kind of high as I would go to meet up with my lover, and then I remember feeling numb and violated when it was over. Many women can relate to this up and down roller coaster ride. In my search for someone to love me, all I found was more pain and more loneliness. I was selling myself short by holding onto this behavior.

Then one day, I was on my knees praying in my prayer closet for about four hours, just sitting and talking with God. I needed answers. I needed to know about this love thing. I didn't know how to connect with people and I didn't know how to love on a deeper level. I didn't know how to show up fully in life and even my children suffered because of this lack of knowledge in me. While in my prayer closet that day, crying and begging God for something … anything...a clue... I felt a warmth suddenly come over me...it was total bliss. For a few moments, everything was perfect...everything felt pure...it felt light, it felt like my heart had found a home. Then I heard God say to me...this is what true love feels like. It was Pure, Unconditional, Wide-Open Love. I simply wept. I had just experienced for the very first time what love looked like. This was yet another defining and life-changing moment for me.

For much of my life, this is what I had hungered for in my soul. To experience what true love felt like. Shortly after the incident in the closet, a radical shift started to happen within my daily experience of life. I learned on that day that we can never find that kind of love in someone else or anything outside of ourselves. It can only be found in our reunification with the True Love Source who is God. God is Love and it's from our reunifying with God that we become the very expression of Love itself.

As we begin to live our lives in deep alignment and oneness with the Greatest Love of All, we will never have to search for anything or anyone to give to us what we can now give to ourselves...self-love. It's this kind of love that can raise our consciousness and the vibration of the planet. It's this kind of love that can break down walls of injustice, crime and hatred. It's from self-love that we can change the planet. God is our Love Source and in reunifying to that Source we have become the very love we seek.

Aligning myself with the Greater Truth of Love was a turning point for me and my life. Learning how to access the limitless source of Love will allow us to live in authentic confidence and faith to bring forth the fulfillment of our greatest potential. We become anchored into the power of true Love.

An amazing thing happened to me once I began to embrace and source my life from Love instead of seeking a man to love me...my soul mate arrived. When we are aligned to, one with, unified with this large field of Love Energy, we gain access to everything we desire and everything we need to bring it forth and make it so. Many of my clients come to me because they want to find true love and their soul mate. I don't begin coaching them on external things as communication techniques, changing their hair or losing weight. I start with helping them to reunify with the Source of Love. When we learn to do this, we become a love magnet and it's just a matter of time before our beloved shows up in our lives. The law of attraction does not lie. Aligning ourselves with the greatest Force of Love in the Universe is the most important choice we can make to bring us complete fulfillment, joy and love.

The love we have been seeking has been there all along. When we search for what we already possess, it's like walking around the house in a panic looking for your keys, not realizing they're already in your hands. Once you realize you are holding your keys, do you continue to look for them? Absolutely not! You immediately begin to use your keys to unlock the door or whatever you need them for.

Once you realize that love already exist within, you can begin looking for ways to share it with the world. Compassion, forgiveness, and peace will become your home. You will begin to live your life from a place of fulfillment instead of need or void, and your life will never be the same!

As part of my daily ritual, I have found that praying and meditating first thing in the morning sets the energetic vibration tone for my day. I find it easy to remember my connection to God and focus on my spiritual identity when I do this ritual. I am now at a place where I know that I am one with God. I didn't say that I had to be perfect; I just needed to believe it so. Learning to make love a lifestyle has become my mission in life. Love is the answer to every question we have in life. If we allow love to be the driving force behind everything we think, say and do, we could literally change the world.

At this writing, I am launching a global movement via the Internet, Social Media and Live Events called, "Take the Vow to Love." Through this movement, I will encourage millions of people globally to take the vow to make love a lifestyle. As we learn to love ourselves and then others, we will change the direction of the planet and make it a better place for all of us. The Love Lifestyle is what I call it, or Flowing in the Love Zone. Let love guide your life and as a result, you will see great things happen.

Summary:
My Second Step to *"My Journey to Being"*: Reunify to Love

My Defining Moment:
Understanding that we can never find true love from anyone or anything outside of ourselves and realizing that God is the True Source of all Love. Therefore, as we reunify with that Source we become the very love we seek

Steps to Reconnecting to Love
1. Seek the Source of Love and not someone or something to love you.
2. Take the vow to love by making love a Lifestyle and allowing it to be the driving force behind all that you think, say and do.
3. Believe that the same Love that created you is the same love that you can become.

Ritual:
Set your daily energetic vibration tone by meditating and praying the very first thing in the morning. Doing this will keep your love energy high and begin attracting all that is good to your life.
Take the vow to love by signing below:
I _____take the vow to make love the driving force behind all that I think, say and do. I take the vow to make love a lifestyle.
Signature_____
Date_____
Learn how you can get involved with this movement by logging onto: www.takethevowtolove.com

4

Release What No Longer Serves You

I once heard someone say, "For things to change, you've got to change." I always thought that for things in my life to change, I had to do things differently. While that may be true, it sounds easier than it is. Each morning I would sit down and make a "to do" list of what I needed to do in order to create change for my life. I would write things like: exercise, take vitamins, read for one hour, return phone calls, balance my check book, call my mother, and tell my children that I love them. I believed in order to make my life better that I had to become more disciplined, more focused, and more committed. Yet, at the end of each day when most of the things on my list didn't get done, I would go to bed feeling defeated and depressed. This cycle would continue until one day I had my "ah ha" moment. I realized that in order for my behavior to change, I had to change the underlying cause of my behavior choices. The under lying causes behind all my behaviors were my thoughts.

I discovered that my "thoughts" were driving my behavior and actions that created the results that I was now experiencing in my daily life. I was busy trying to change what I was doing, but what I should have been doing was transforming what I was thinking.

Our patterns of thoughts are directly related to the beliefs that were programmed in us at a young age. As I said before, most of our emotional and mental programming is formed in us by the time we are eight years of age. If your life experiences taught you that this is an unsafe world because the people who were suppose to care for

23

you only wounded and hurt you, then the beliefs you hold for your life will always come from a place of fear and self-protection. When a father doesn't clearly communicate to his daughter that she can count on him to protect her and meet her needs, she forms a belief inside of her that says, "those who love you can't be trusted or depended upon."

As a fatherless daughter, I never had the honor of feeling protected or secure by my father. This resulted in me learning to be self-reliant and self-protected. These behaviors were interpreted by others as me being unapproachable, distant or not needing anything from anyone. All those years of my grandmother calling me names, years of feeling abandoned by my father and years of feeling disconnected from my mom created a belief in me that said I was insignificant and that I was invisible. Somewhere in my subconscious mind, these beliefs created an invisible barrier around my ability to form meaningful relationships with others; even with my husband and children. Beliefs are formed early in life and they are formed without any filters of reasoning or logic. They are purely emotionally charged and that's what makes them so powerful.

With a belief that the people in my life weren't dependable, I tried to make sure that I would always be dependable. My focus became solely about by trying to please everyone else and meet their needs. Never wanting to disappoint anyone when asked to do something, my answer would always be "yes", even when I wanted to say no. When someone did something to hurt me, I wouldn't stand up for myself and I went along with whatever they wanted of me because I didn't want to cause trouble, create conflict or have them angry with me.

I would not express any physical signs of being hurt or angry, but on the inside I would be seething with rage. Rage is the hallmark trait of a Fatherless Daughter, but anger is not a natural state for us as humans. Rage is a learned emotion that keeps us out of alignment with our truest selves. I remember one day my ex-husband didn't come home until 4am in the morning. It was one of those nights when he was with one of his mistresses. When I began to question him about where he'd been, he tried to run a huge guilt trip on me. He gave me a lame story about how he was not with anyone, but he was riding around all night thinking about how bad our marriage had become. I knew he was lying, but I didn't want him to think that I was insecure, so I accepted his lame excuse. As I walked away from the conversation, I had a smile on my face, but inside I was so angry that I could have punched him in his face. After years of allowing folks to do what they wanted to me, my internal dialogue became filled with many toxic thoughts. These thoughts were influencing my behavior and choices which resulted in unfavorable life experiences.

My defining moment was when I realized that the true source of my pain was not what others did to me, but the true source of my pain was my inability to forgive, to be honest and to let go. I would sit in church and hear messages on forgiveness, but no one ever told me how to forgive others. I knew that in order for me to ever begin living life differently, I had to forgive those who had wounded me. The forgiveness was no longer about them, it had become about me and my destiny. When we don't forgive, it's as if we are trying to move forward with shackles on our feet that are anchored and bolted to the ground. When we try to lift our feet up off the ground, nothing can happen. We remain stuck in our past, trying to move towards the future. Forgiveness allows us to step out of our history into a brighter and promising future.

Forgiveness releases us from the shackles of the pain and the wounds that were inflicted upon us. I wanted so much for my life to be different and if it meant letting go of what others had done to me, it would be well worth it. Forgiveness is a decision to let go of any resentment, anger or thoughts of revenge. Forgiveness starts with the decision to forgive, and also with us accepting responsibility for whom and what we allowed to hurt us. We must also forgive ourselves for how we have showed up in life as a victim of our circumstances. The life that I wanted to experience became greater than my need to remain a wounded victim because the "wounded victim" mentality no longer served who I wanted to be. Realizing and understanding that no matter what other people may have done to you, it is still your choice to forgive them, rise above it and take control of your own destiny. I took control of my life by letting go and releasing what no longer served me.

One day I decided to sit on the floor with paper and pen and write down everyone I could think of who had hurt, offended and wounded me. The list was getting so long until I stopped and took a good look at the list and then I asked myself, "Really Angela? Did all of these people wake up one day and decide to make your life miserable?" It was in that moment I realized that a lot of what I assumed were offenses directed towards me, were really my perspective on things and the way I viewed life as a whole. Because of my "Fatherless Daughter" issues, I tended to view life through the tainted lenses of rejection, victimization and abandonment.

I forgave myself for judging others who hurt me. I also needed to do the work to eliminate the sabotaging thoughts and beliefs that no longer served me. These patterns of beliefs were impacting the way life was showing up in my daily experiences. I am not saying that everything that was done to me was not real or valid, but there were some people on my list who really should not have been there. When choosing to forgive others, it is important that we also search our own hearts and minds for ways in which we might have helped to create, attract or influence the offenses. Much of what we experience could be a result of what we've been thinking. As we practice the art of forgiveness, it lifts us above all of the pain and chaos to a space whereby we can see clearly the power of true vision.

After I completed my list, I called out loud each person's name on the list and said, "I forgive you for _____ and I release you from your offense." When I was done, I tore up the list and burned it. This was a ritual, but something on the inside of me shifted into a new experience of what true freedom was. As I watched the fire burn the paper, I also watched my past burn away.

Sure there will be days when you see your offender and you begin to feel a little uneasy. But if you remain focused on how bright your future is because of your willingness to forgive, the need to remain angry or hurt will begin to dissipate. When we focus more on the power and the results of forgiveness in our personal lives, the need to hold someone to their mistakes, to their senseless offenses becomes null and void. I wanted more for my life, and if letting go was the answer, I was willing to raise my hands.

As time passed, I truly began to feel lighter. I could speak of a person who had once hurt me, and I didn't feel any pain. Then forgiveness began to turn into compassion. When I learned that wounded people wound other people, that news liberated me. I knew then that most of the folks who had done these things to me had been wounded themselves and I obviously had wounded some folks myself.

If we believe that the world is unsafe, our actions and behaviors will always come from a place of fear and protection. When we come from a place of fear we vibrate a low level energetically. Everything that exists is made up of energy, even you and I. If we were to place an ink pen under the best microscope, we would see the energy vibrating from it. We, as humans, are much the same. We are either vibrating from a place of love or fear. The root of every thought or emotional feeling that you have derives from fear based thoughts and beliefs or love based thoughts and beliefs. If your thoughts and beliefs are fear based, they may show up in your life disguised as anger, resentment, scarcity, sickness and lack. If your thoughts are love based, they may show up in your life disguised as happiness, joy, abundances and intimacy. The root of all experiences in life will be generated from fear or love.

Our energy or vibration goes out into the Universe and seeks a matching vibration. When it finds its vibration match, that match is then manifested in our lives. For example, if your thoughts or beliefs are, "I'm always broke, or no one will ever love me", your energetic vibration goes out to the universe to seek its match and it will return back to you in many forms that represents lack; such as a huge medical bill, a job loss, a lover who is emotionally unavailable or a divorce. The universe will always return to you what you want and what you want is what you are vibrating. So when you think and feel, "I am lovable and I am abundantly rich," your vibration goes out to the universe to find a match. It shows up in your life in many ways; such as an unexpected raise on your job or a check in the mail, a new man in your life or a renewed marriage.

Everything in life is created by a single thought. When our feelings accompany the thoughts, they intensify the vibration and attract to us a perfect match. This law of attraction principle has taught me that I could literally change my life on purpose. But how can we have positive thoughts in our lives when most of what we've been programmed for has been negative?

There are numerous ways of doing this and I have had tremendous success with many of my clients through using several techniques and processes. Some of the things you can start doing right away are reading personal growth materials, hanging around positive people, mediation, and prayer. These new actions became my new ritual. I read numerous books with powerful quotes. I memorized those quotes and said them aloud to myself in the mirror. One of my mentors gave me a pre-loaded IPod with hours of powerful inspirational and empowering presentations and speakers. I would listen to them every single day. I began removing negative people and influences from my life such as: negative television shows and music. I started meditating daily and something magical happened. The meditation began erasing many of my old thoughts.

Then one day something happened that caught my attention. I was dating a guy who was a few years younger than I. He called and said that he was going out of town with some friends and I said "Okay." Remember, I usually said "Okay" even when I didn't mean it. But this time when I hung up the phone, I really didn't feel any bad feelings. In the past, because of my fatherless daughter abandonment and rejection issues, I would have questioned him about who he was going with, how long he would be gone, where were they going and what would they be doing? Ladies, you know the drill. I also would have been depressed the entire time he was gone, wondering what he was doing and who he was doing it with. But this time, I really felt fine. When I said "Okay" I really meant it. And it was then that I discovered the key to changing my life. I could not change it by doing things differently; I had to "be" different. All those months of forgiveness, letting go, erasing old thoughts and replacing new ones had shifted who I was becoming at my core. My thoughts changed effortlessly and so did my behavior.

This kind of change is not about using willpower or sheer might, but it is must become an internal shift from deep within. Nothing in life can happen externally until it happens internally first. It really is more about who you are being instead of what you are doing.

Living from a place of love and not fear, I now understood that I didn't have to try to protect myself because I was already being supported and protected by God. Sure, changing our thoughts can change our lives, but it must first begin with a decision to forgive. Forgiveness is the key that unlocks the door to change, transformation and renewal. Once you have released the old, you can begin to make room for the new. Nowadays, I don't make a "To Do" list; I read, study, and meditate to shift into becoming that which I seek.

Summary:
The third step to "My Journey to Being": Release What No Longer Serves You.

My Defining Moment:
Realizing that the source of my pain was not what others did to me, but it was my inability to forgive them and let go. By accepting the fact that forgiveness releases me from the shackles of the pain and wounds that were inflicted upon me, forgiveness became my ticket to freedom.

Steps to Releasing What No Longer Serves You:
1.   Make a decision to forgive and unlock the door to change and transformation in your life.
2.   Decide to stop playing the victim and move to a space of being victorious in life.
3.   Understand that changing your thoughts is the key to changing your behavior, not willpower.
4.   Remember to forgive yourself.

My Ritual:
Make a list of everyone who has wounded or hurt you. Then ask yourself if what you perceived was actually an offense from each person or if the pain was due to your tainted thinking of victimhood. Go through each name on the list and declare out loud that you forgive him/her for the offense. Once you have done this, burn the list and release all the emotional pain as you watch the fire burn. When needed, remind yourself of the day you released the pain and forgave your offenders and yourself.

5
Recover What You Gave Away

He didn't speak to me for over a year. He told me that I had destroyed his life. He said that I never believed in him. He said that I didn't support his dreams and he said that I was a horrible person. I heard the words and I felt the pain for a moment. These words did not come from a boyfriend or my husband, but from my son. That's right! They were words filled with anger, rage and pain and they were directed towards me. As I sat there and listened through the phone, I dared not say anything for fear he would hang up and never speak to me again. So I allowed him to speak and he did – for three and a half hours. I started out sitting on the chair as I listened, then I moved to sitting on the floor, and by the time he was done telling me off, I was lying on my back with the phone just lying there next to my ears because my arms became tired from holding the receiver.

My son was twenty seven years of age at the time and he was very angry with me. He felt that I had not been a great mom. And to a certain degree, I agreed with him. When I was married to my children's father, I was a broken, lost and confused young woman who desperately wanted to be loved in a world where love appeared not to exist for me. I was wounded, depressed and unhappy. My ex-husband, their father, and I were young and we both didn't know how to make love work. He was broken, I was broken. When we got married, he was twenty one and I was seventeen. We barely knew how to write a check, yet alone make a marriage work and become parents. At the age of nineteen, I gave birth to our first child and by the time I was twenty three I had given birth to our third child. Imagine, twenty three years old, married with three children, struggling financially, emotionally bankrupt and trying to make life work? It was a disaster waiting to happen and the only people who suffered the most were the kids.

When I think back, I believe I kept having children because I wanted to be loved, and babies offer love back to us so unconditionally. Yet through my brokenness and fear that the world was an unsafe place, I subjected my children to a life of sheer smothering, control and, in many ways, fear. I wanted them to be perfect because I held a belief that "If I am perfect, they won't leave me, and they will love me." I believed, at that time, if my children were perfect they would never have to endure the things I did in my life. We can never ensure what someone else's path in life will be, especially our children's. The only demonstration of a care taker for me was my grandmother who emotionally tormented me. Wounded as I was, I regretfully looked back and realize that I did the same thing to my own kids. While two of them would disagree and never say that I was a bad mother, I know that I caused great emotional pain in all of their lives. Only my son dared to tell me the truth.

When my ex-husband left, I became a single mother of two teenage sons and one daughter; and fear gripped me like a noose around my neck. I was determined that my sons would not end up in jail or in gangs and my daughter would not have a bunch of baby daddies. I thought I could ensure that belief by keeping them under lock and key and under my 'mommy dearest' control. I had to be brutal and it was necessary, so I thought. I had inflicted the fear of God in those three kids by Bible-whipping them and taking them to churches where the pastor did the same. It's a wonder that they don't hate all Bible-toting church going folks.

My entire life became consumed with my kids. Every breath I took, every decision I made, every action step I took, I did it with them in mind. I lived to be their mother and I was going to make sure they were perfect in every sense of the word. But I would later discover that I broke and wounded them instead. In my attempt to love them, I had given away all of whom I was and who I could become; and it almost cost them the opportunity to be who they were meant to be. I felt that because I provided a nice home, nice clothes, food on the table, and took them to church that I was a great mother. I was the parent who stayed with them and paid for everything and took them to all of their extracurricular activities, took care of their illnesses, endured all those boring PTA meetings, school concerts, plays, baseball games, recitals, and helped with homework. I treated them as if I deserved some type of "Medal of Honor" because I didn't desert them and they needed to repay me for the rest of their lives with gratitude and appreciation. Wow, little did I know that was not how they were interpreting it and feeling it at all.

We can never undo the damage that we have done to our kids. I will never be able to take away the pain that I inflicted upon their lives. No, my sons didn't join gangs or go to jail and my daughter didn't have any baby daddies, but they did suffer with low self-esteem, struggled in relationships and struggled with loving themselves. They saw the world as unsafe and they allowed limitations to be placed on their lives. I had actually become to them what my grandmother was to me and I will forever thank them for still loving me anyway.

Thank God for His mercy and grace that allowed me to expand and to grow before I departed this earth. It has given me the opportunity to have since apologized to each of them and do my best to make it right by being a better mother and grandmother. I am so very proud of each of them and they are exactly as they should be and who they should be in spite of all my craziness.

I now know that I could not have given to them what I didn't have myself. Love is what they needed and I was looking for it through my children. As fatherless daughters, we will search and grab hold of love anywhere we can find it. I was still angry with their father for not stepping up and doing his part, angry because I had to raise them alone, angry because my daughter would be a fatherless daughter like me. I was fearful that I would not get it right and what I feared did happen… I didn't get it right on so many levels.

I'd given up my rights, my power and who I really was to anyone who asked. I walked into a marriage and into motherhood with an empty tank. We can only give to others out of our overflow, the full cup is for ourselves and an empty cup serves no one. Until we recover what we have given away, we can never give to others because you can't give what you don't have. I simply could not give love because I had none to give. Admitting to myself that I was worthy of getting my lost self back was the first step to my recovery. When we come into this world, all that we need and all that we are meant to become is perfect. We enter this world completely loved; completely perfect; and a perfect image in the mind of God.

In acknowledging that I was worthy of recovering it all, I began to recover my lost self and renew my relationship with Angela. What did I want? What did I like? What was my favorite color, favorite movie, my favorite food? I had given away so many parts of myself until I couldn't even answer the smallest of questions. While trying to be a perfect daughter, a perfect grand-daughter, a perfect sister, a perfect wife and a perfect mother, I literally gave away who I was actually meant to be. No one can be all things to all people, we can only be who we really are; and that is enough.

I began to spend an enormous amount of time in isolation to regroup, renew and recover. During this time I recognized that my attempt to get others to love me was really me sacrificing my truest self and giving away my authentic power. It's never okay to ask someone to do for you what you are not willing or capable of doing for yourself.

As a ritual, I began to ask myself, "What have you given away?" Then I made a list of all the things that I felt I had given away. By organizing myself around what others wanted from me, without establishing healthy boundaries, I somehow felt a need to please and give them what they wanted. When we redirect our focus towards ourselves and really believe that we deserve to have our own needs met, this becomes the first step to recovering all that we've given away. I recovered love and I discovered "me."

In smothering my children with my fear based parenting attitude, I created for them a life of uncertainty and insecurity that continued into their adulthood. As my children got older and began moving out of the house to live life on their own, one of the things they all became good at was asking me for money. While I do believe in helping our children as they begin their lives, there is a limit to what we should be doing. But just like I did with my love, I did with my money the same way. Because how we "do" love is how we "do" money. I gave my children money that I didn't have. Meaning I would not pay my own obligations in order to pay theirs; even when they took their money and wasted it. I gave every time they would ask until I was beginning to believe that I was a walking ATM. But all good mothers give their money to their adult children, right? Wrong. What I was doing was trying to win their love and get them to see me as a perfect and better mom than I was when they were growing up. My belief had now become, if I say "no" then they won't love me. Again, I was giving away my power. I learned that I was willing to lose my own power by not meeting my obligations in order to meet the obligations of my children. This mindset didn't serve me and it disempowered them. Once again, I had to hold myself powerful and say "no." Saying no was not easy at first. But saying "no" to my children allowed me to stand in integrity with my creditors and to allow my children to stand in their own power as well. This kind of "no" served everyone. But more importantly it allowed me to understand that I deserved to stand powerfully and I could at any moment choose "me."

As women, we give so much of ourselves away because we hold a case of mistaken identity about who we are. Trying to get others to love, acknowledge and value us by pleasing and meeting their needs only has cost us much pain and suffering. In my pursuit to recover, we need to remember that we are one with God. Understanding and acknowledging this makes us all powerful and magnificent. While I would have never intentionally set out to destroy my children's lives, I now know that I made them more important than myself. I also realized that I was born to be more than a mother. My life's purpose was not just to be their mother; there was so much more to me than motherhood. I love being a mother, but motherhood is no longer my primary reason for existence. I know many moms will perhaps cringe when you read this, and I hope you do. I hope you do feel the discomfort, because making your children your highest priority in life will place you out of divine right order. I now have a divine right order in my life. It's when we don't have a real knowledge of divine right order, we get confused; and a confused mind always says "no." Please understand that I am not saying or advocating neglecting our children. I merely mean that when you love yourself first, it becomes easier to love your kids because you now understand what love truly is and you are giving to your children from a full cup instead of an empty one. My children now have the uncanny responsibility to make life better for themselves.

Many of us may have had damaging things done to us, but it is still our responsibility to forgive, repair and let go. There are times, however, when some relationships will never be repaired. It's when we must tell ourselves the truth about who people really are. Maya Angelo once said, "When people show you who they are, let them."

As I mentioned earlier in this book, my niece and nephew came to live with us when I was nine years old. My relationship with my niece had always been strained. For some reason, and I have never been able to figure it out, she has always had it in for me. You would think that I should be the one who had a problem with her, but that's simply not the case. I always felt a sense of protection for her because I knew her story and I never wanted her to ever experience what she had endured again. My niece and I are only four years apart in age and reared in the same household, but we don't associate with each other outside of family gatherings. She has gone out of her way to make it clear to me that she does not like me. I have never been able to figure out what the issue is and for over forty years I kept silent and took whatever she would dish out to me. After reaching out to her in many ways, I came to the conclusion that this relationship will never be healed. When she refused to attend my wedding I still reached out. When she refused to attend a special birthday celebration, I still reached out to her. When she refused to come to my house once I married my new husband, I still reached out. When she told lies about me to people who knew me, I still reached out to her. I love my niece and I always will, but I finally had to ask myself an important question, "What in me believes that it's okay to allow her to treat you this way?" When I heard myself say these words, I simply chose to let it go. In that moment I took back my power, reclaimed my truth and gave her back to herself.

There will be times in your life when no matter what you do, people will not like you. Instead of playing the victim and trying to figure out the reason why, you simply have to let it go. See them as they can be and not as they are; until then love them from where they are. Loving my niece from a space of deep compassion and giving her back to herself has freed me from years of pressure and burdens. We all have to tell the truth all the time. And sometimes the truth means that you cannot share the same space with a person in order to truly love them. In our journey to repair the damage that has been done to us, it must never start with your offenders or abusers. It always starts with you. It's never about the other person and this rift between my niece and I, it is not about her. It really is about how I choose to see her and how I choose to respond to her. It's about whether or not I will respond in love or in fear. I choose love. Because I don't know the answer to why this issue exists between us, I am absolutely sure that Love is the answer to every question. For now this is how the story goes, but who knows what Love will do to change it?

I have shared this same truth with my own children and they now realize that they are responsible for their own destiny and they can no longer play the victim. In my son's outburst to blame me for his life's problems, he also realized that all he can ever expect from me is an "I'm sorry." In my attempt to be a good mother, I sacrificed myself and in return hurt my children. This is exactly what happens when you try to give from an empty cup. It really does not benefit anyone.

We can never go back and redo our lives or change the way it played out. All anyone can do is offer an apology, learn and grow. I have given my children to themselves and now they all have the choice to forgive and repair their lives. I have given my niece back to herself and she has a choice to forgive, release and let go as well. I will not remain nailed to the cross of my past, I will stand up for who and what I am and I will show up in life as a bigger and a more expanded version of myself.

I'd like to think that I have a very good relationship with my children now, yet I may never have a good relationship with my niece. But what I know for sure and what I have learned is that I do everyone a disservice by loving them more than loving myself. It's time to take back your power, recover what you gave away, reclaim your right to exist and give love to yourself.

Summary:

The fourth step to "My Journey to Being": Recover What You Gave Away.

My Defining Moment

Realizing that I give to others out of my overflow, I give to myself out of a full cup, and an empty cup serves no one.

Steps to Recovering What You Gave Away:

1. Make yourself a priority in your divine right order of life.

2. Never give to others what you are not willing or capable of giving to yourself too.

3. Do not allow your mistakes to keep you nailed to the cross of the past.

Ritual

Make a list of what you have given away. How did you give away your power and who did you give it to? Then list ways in which you can recover it.

_____

_____

_____

_____

_____

_____

_____

_____

_____

_____

_____

_____

6

Reactivate Your Life

For over twenty one years, I had the pleasure of working with kids and teenagers through my Modeling and Performing Arts Company. It was a great career and I had many success stories. Nothing is as pure as being a part of shaping a child's dream and seeing it become a reality. While I loved the work and enjoyed it tremendously, I knew there was more that I had to do in my life. As a child, I always felt that I was invisible and that no one saw me. So I spent my time at my company providing a stage on which kids could perform and see and hear the applause. I wanted them to know that we see them. I wanted them to know that we hear them and that we acknowledge them. But still I always knew there was more for me to do.

Over the years, I formed some very special relationships with the mothers of my students. It was as if we had some kind of magical connection. I discovered that many women were hurting and suffering. I knew that pain because I had lived it all my life. They would share with me their pains, their struggles and their fears. I would share with them my advice and on several occasions we would all cry together. Soon I started hosting and facilitating workshops for women. Little did I know this path would lead me to where I am today. The workshops were incredible and the results were amazing. One day I received a phone call from one of the workshop attendees, who I will call Joan. Joan had brought her girlfriend to one of my workshops. Joan told me that her friend said that I had saved her life. The day the friend came to my workshop was the day she had decided to commit suicide, but she chose to attend this one last event with Joan because she wanted to see her again. She was going to still kill herself after the workshop. She continued to share that what I said during the workshop gave her hope to live. I was floored! I could not believe that my workshop had saved someone's life. Yet, I still didn't get it. Early on in this journey of personal growth, I had penned a little booklet called, "The Revival of a Love Story...7 Steps to Finding True Love." I gave it to friends and family because it really was something that I wrote for myself as a way of healing and purging. One day I received a call from a friend saying that his neighbors were going through a very difficult time in their marriage and one evening they got into a huge fight. He shared with me that he had taken my little booklet to the couple's house and sat down with them at the kitchen table and they read it together and discussed it. He told me that night saved that couple's marriage. But I still didn't get it. So one day I received a card in the mail from someone in Virginia. The card said that my mother had given them my little booklet and he and his fiancé read it together. He shared with me how it changed their perspectives on love and helped to deepen their love for one another. I still didn't get it. Then I held a women's circle at my studio for a friend of mine whose mentor was coming to town. We invited a group of ladies and we had a very powerful time. My friend's mentor spoke into my life about the work that I was doing. She told me that I was doing "life work", as she put it. I didn't quite understand what she was saying because I was merely working with kids in my performing arts center. She also told me what my business colors would be. I thought she was perhaps a little off. I still didn't get it.

You may be asking yourself, "What didn't she get?" I didn't get that God and the universe were sending me clues. We all come into this world with a purpose and a mission. I used to believe that our purpose was what we loved and enjoyed doing and would do even if we didn't get paid for it. I now believe that our purpose in life will be directly connected to our pain in life. Whatever has been our biggest struggle and our biggest pain becomes our purpose in life to help others heal from. All of my life I have struggled with love. Loving myself and wondering if anyone would ever love me was my single biggest pain in life. This thing called "love" had caused me the most pain in life. I just could not seem to get a handle on it. I didn't know what love looked like.

Now I know that the love I searched for in others, in food, and in shopping was already within me. It was there all the time. I also know that deep down inside, we all want the same thing. As I was searching for love, I found it within me and my oneness with God. And it is because of this journey, that my true purpose in life unfolded. I was born to learn this lesson and I was born to teach it to other women, especially those women who didn't have a close emotional bond with their fathers. I am specifically drawn to fatherless daughters because that was where my inability to love myself started. This is what I've been assigned to do. Some call it "Finding Your Purpose," but I call it, "Finding my Sweet Spot". I can assure you that I did not coin that word. But it sure does sound right and it feels good to find your sweet spot. I believe that your sweet spot is an intersection between who you are and what you are here to do. Who I am is love, I was born to love, and I am here to teach others about love. When I discovered my sweet spot, the desire to continue what I was doing previously began to fade. I just didn't have the zeal and the heart for it any longer. I loved the work that I did with the kids. I loved the performing arts world and the entertainment business. But not only do I love what I do now, I am so passionate about it that I am willing to die for it. Why? Because I don't want another woman, another fatherless daughter, to live a life of mistaken identity and never knowing what love is.

One day I walked into my performing arts studio of twenty one years and in a moment, I got it. I realized in that moment that this journey had ended. I grabbed my handbag, called the guy who owned the building, paid up my rent and walked out. I have never been back. I didn't even move my things. A friend of mine went and moved all of my stuff. Even now, I don't know where it is stored.

There was something stirring inside of me and I wasn't quite clear what it was. I needed to understand what was trying to emerge through me. I began to seek out mentors, life coaches and people who could help me. And they did. I realized that I had taken myself as far as I could alone. I needed help. That was a defining moment for me. I could not walk this path alone and I didn't have to. There were people who genuinely wanted to help me, people who saw in me what I could not see in myself. For the first time in my life, I knew and experienced what it meant to be cared for, to be looked after, to be coached, and to be mentored. It changed my life. Little did I know that I would be doing the same for others; "Life Work" as the lady said.

As we begin to step fully into our life's purpose, our lives become fully reactivated. To reactivate means to activate or renew an old file. Somehow my original file had gotten lost or hidden within all the pain and chaos in my life. But as my life began to unfold and my truest, authentic self began to surface, so did my true purpose in life. It was always there and always will be because it is an undeletable file. It will never go away. Your true mission in life, your true purpose in life, can never be deleted. It can remain inactive for years. Many people die and never see their dreams and purpose actualized. Don't let this happen to you. It's never too late to discover your sweet spot. It took me over twenty one years of doing something else to discover my true life's work. I don't regret any part of my journey. Those years of working with the kids was training. I learned a lot about business, how to deal with people and how to operate as a professional. Working with young people also helped to open my heart because they love so unconditionally. All those years, my students held me up with their love.

Now that I have reactivated my life, nothing has remained the same. Every day I get to work with women from around the world and help them unlock the hidden secrets to transforming their relationships with men and money. These were two areas that seemed to be a struggle for me. I couldn't manage or sustain loving relationships and I couldn't manage or sustain financial success. One of the reasons for this was due to my fatherless daughter syndrome. The two primary needs of a young girl are love and security and if these two needs are **NOT** met early on in a girl's life, as she approaches womanhood she begins to judge her life's success and her self-worth based on the money she earns and the emotional state of her relationships.

I learned to shift this belief and I now help women from around the world do the same through my Love Lifestyle Coaching System. I am flowing in the "Love Zone," working from my sweet spot and it is totally awesome!! When we reactivate our lives, it tends to have a domino effect.

Most of us sit and wait on life's emergencies to happen, which forces us to find our purpose in life. Sometimes our purpose will find us through painful circumstances. However, we can have an emergence without an emergency when we realize how much the world needs our help. Your gifts want to emerge now. You are full of possibility and potential. Don't wait until you lose your job to start that new business. You don't have to wait until you get sick to begin living and teaching healthy living seminars. Your teenage daughter does not have to become pregnant for you to start a personal development program for young girls.

No, don't wait until life's emergency forces you to emerge, do it now. Not only will your life become powerful, but you will impact and transform the lives of others. It is destined to happen!!

Summary:
The fifth step to *"My Journey to Being"*: Reactivate Your Life.

My Defining Moment:
Realizing that in order to move my life forward and fulfill my true purpose in life I had to find a mentor and coach to be successful. I realized that I could not take this journey alone, nor did I have to.

Steps to Reactivating Your Life:
1. Discover Your True Purpose in Life.
2. Begin working from Your Sweet Spot.
3. Find a mentor or coach

Ritual:
This is a great exercise in discovering your true purpose in life. What has been the single biggest pain and struggle in your life?

_____

_____

_____

_____

What makes you angry about what is happening in the world today?

_____

_____

_____

_____

What are you good at doing? Writing, Speaking, Drawing, Singing, Organizing, etc.?

_____

_____

_____

_____

_____

Whatever has been your single biggest pain and makes you angry, you are here to help solve it in the world. You will use your talents, gifts and what you are good at as a vehicle to bring about the solutions. What would that vision look like? Write it down below:

_____

_____

_____

_____

_____

_____

_____

_____

_____

_____

_____

_____

_____

_____

_____

_____

_____

_____

_____

_____

7

Reestablish Your Place in the World

At the writing of this manuscript, I have never traveled out of the country except to the Bahamas. But I have many friends and clients who have lived all over the world. My husband has traveled the world and I have promised him that I will begin this year. When you have only seen the world from just one perspective or one corner, you have a limited view of what the world is like. I know this and that is why I have decided to start traveling more this year, especially out of the country. While I may not have left the US, I had a global awakening a few years ago. And it was at that moment my view of the world began to change.

I was in a meeting with a friend who is from Iran. She was speaking about love and being connected to the God and to each other. She candidly said "Many Christians criticize those who don't speak the name of Jesus. But do you know that there are people in my country who have never heard of Jesus...?" Now you would think that I already knew this; and on some level I did. But to hear her say it in her accent and with such passion and concern for how we do not love each other, it struck a nerve in me. I do believe in the Deity of Christ and I am a Christian, but her statement changed something within me. I no longer see the world through a singular view of "us and them". I know I don't have all of the answers and there's a lot I don't understand. But what I know for sure is that I must see the world as God sees it and not the way man has filtered it through his own interpretation for much economic gain.

We live in a big and huge world that God has created and this I now know for sure. I have brothers and sisters everywhere and what has connected us all is God and His Love. Who am I to say that I have all the answers and how can I say if you don't agree with my answers then you are doomed? I may be powerful, but not that powerful. We have been placed in this world to make a difference. Martin Luther King did. Gandhi did. Mother Teresa did. Nelson Mandela, Oprah, and Obama are all doing it. Not only did they make a difference, they hold a global world view of how we all should love and respect each other.

In a world where love is not the fundamental premise for how we do anything, there must be a reestablishing of it if we as a species are going to survive. To reestablish simply means to bring back into the original existence. This entire universe was created from love, for love, by love. That has been and always will be the original intent for its existence. Somehow, we as the human species have allowed hatred and fear to rule the world. While I know we can't all be the Gandhi's of the world, we can do as he has instructed us, "Be the change you want to see in the world".

Love is the answer to every question, every situation or circumstance. When I learned the power of love and what love could do, I knew it was time to reestablish my place in the world. My place is the "Love Zone". The "Love Zone" is where God and I exist as one. This is and always has been mine and your authentic and original existence. Every time we have ever experienced pain, discord, discomfort or problems, it was because we forgot to flow in the "Love Zone". In order to reestablish our place in the world, we must first reestablish love in our own lives.

As I began to understand what it meant to see the world as God sees it, I could no longer watch the clips on television of the world's disasters and not be moved. Before then I could walk past the television and see and not be moved because it was not close to home. I was so caught up in my own life and my own issues that I had forgotten to care. But when love is activated in your life and you begin living in the "Love Zone", you cannot help but seek out ways to make a difference. Making a difference will always start with you becoming the difference you want to create. If love is going to heal the world, then it would stand to reason that each of us must make a commitment to become the love that heals. Actually, returning to our original state is what I mean by becoming love.

When we talk about making a difference, most people think I am speaking of doing something large and off the charts. Absolutely not! In the Bible when God gave Moses the command to deliver the children of Israel out of Pharaoh's hands, Moses offered God excuses as to why he couldn't do it. But God asked Moses a question that I think all of us need to answer, "What's in your hands?" What do you have in your hands right now that will enable you to take action in order to create a better world? Many of us are gifted with enormous talents to use in ways which could bring so much good to the planet. The only thing that is standing between you and your dream is your next step. The dream becomes alive and powerful when you just do it. We all have a responsibility to use our talents to make a contribution to make this a better world.

I want to encourage you to take an inventory of what you already have in your possession. Perhaps you don't have the money to start that new business. But you can offer a free workshop to an organization or company that will give you the opportunity to introduce your services and products. Maybe you don't have the money to record your new song, but you do have the vocals to sing free at the next community event. Just like with Moses, when you begin to use what's in your hands, God will add power and miracles to your efforts which will always produce success! Moses was motivated by love to fulfill his mission, and so it is with us. In all that we do, our aim must be to create a world filled with love.

Love is transforming and renewing. I have seen it work and I have experienced the power of it. One day my husband was very upset with me about something, I can't even remember what it was, but he was furious. It had to have been serious because he went in the bedroom and wouldn't come out. I remember thinking to myself that the only way to diffuse this is to apply love. So I walked into the bedroom and I said to him, "I love you." He looked at me like he wanted to argue. He started fussing and I walked up to him and hugged him and kissed him. He wanted to argue and remain angry, but I stood strongly on love's ground...in the "Love Zone". He melted and he reciprocated, "I love you too." I watched love win. So then I began applying it to other things. When I mistakenly pull out in front of someone's car or make a wrong turn and they honk the horn and shout out of the window, I put my hands together in a prayer sign and move my lips in the motion to say "I'm so sorry". Most of the responses I receive back are them immediately grabbing their steering wheel and looking straight ahead with their mouths closed. Love diffused the anger. I have learned that in the midst of love; hate, fear and anger cannot exist. It's impossible for love and fear to exist together.

We can literally change the planet when we take the vow to love. That's what I decided to do in reestablishing my place in the world. At this writing, I am in the midst of starting a global movement whereby I will use the power of the Internet to encourage and inspire others to log onto my site (www.takethevowtolove.com) and take the vow to love. I will use the site to teach about global change through the power of love. Finding my "sweet spot" allowed me to reactivate my life and now that I am restored back to my original existence, I can now reestablish my place in the world by becoming the love that I am and expanding it to the world. What will you do to spread love? In doing so, you will reestablish who you are in the world; and that my friend, is very powerful.

Summary:

The sixth step to "My Journey to Being": Re-establish Your Place in the World.

My Defining Moment:

When I realized that no one person has all of the answers to life's questions, but Love does answer all.

3 Steps to Re-establishing Yourself in the World:

1. Discover what you can do to become a change maker.
2. Become the change you wish to see in the world.
3. Do it now and don't delay

Ritual:

How will you use your life to make a difference in your community, town, state, nation or world? What can you do to become the change you want to see in the world? Write it below and then share it with your mentor/coach to come up with a strategic plan. Give your plan a timeline and a launch date.

_____

_____

_____

_____

_____

_____

_____

_____

_____

_____

_____

_____

_____

_____

_____

_____

8
Rewrite Your Own Love Story

I was sitting at the foot of my bed, crying and having one of my many "pity parties". I was so lonely. I just wanted someone to love me. My ex-husband and I had divorced and he was re-married. I was watching "A Wedding Story" on TLC and after about three episodes, I exploded into tears. I wanted the fairy tale love story that those brides had. I wondered what was wrong with me. I had dated some, but nothing was anything worth talking about. I wanted a mutually meaningful, loving, intimate relationship. It was in the midst of this pity party, that I heard a small whisper, "Revive Your Own Love Story". Now I knew that the word "revive" meant to bring back to life, but what love story did I have to bring back? I knew God didn't mean for it to be with my ex-husband because that was far from a love story.

The answer became clear that my love story must begin with me. I had spent years trying to get others to do for me, what I needed to do for myself. Learning to love myself from a deeper place became my mission. How would I do this? I thought about the things that I did to fall in love with someone else such as spending time with that person and getting to know him. So in my attempt to fall in love with me, I began to spend time with myself. It was about reviving my own love story. Only what I was not giving in this situation was missing; I was not loving myself. I wanted someone else to do for me what I was not willing to do for myself. I wanted someone else to love me, when I wasn't willing to love myself. And that is a very unkind thing to do to anyone. So my journey to finding true love began.

The first thing I did in my quest to love me more, was take off all of my clothes and stand in front of a full length mirror. I had to look at every single part of my imperfect body and see it as perfect. Then I leaned in closer to look into my eyes. If you decide to do this yourself, don't be surprise at the uneasy feeling you experience at first. The first time I did this ritual, I had an intense urge to stop it and not go on with it, but I pushed pass the fear. As I leaned into the mirror and looked myself squarely in the eyes, I said to myself, "Angela, I love you." It felt strange at first. So I did it again, while still looking into the mirror up close I said, "Angela, I love you." The second time felt a little better.

I repeated this process seven times. Each time I did it, it felt a little better. This became a daily ritual as I would get out of the shower. I found a small hand mirror in the store that had written on it "Hello Beautiful" and I purchased it. When I am combing my hair and have to look at the back of my head, I hold that mirror in front of me and each time, I say "Hello Beautiful". This mirror ritual created an opening within my heart where I could begin to allow love to easily flow towards myself. I was reviving my own love story and it really did begin with me. Little changes and shifts in my behavior such as buying myself fresh flowers each week and treating myself to long, soothing baths with candles and a little soft jazz. Writing in my journal of how wonderful and loving I was became a regular routine for me. I began to really enjoy my alone time. Not because I wanted to be away from people or because I was sad, but because I was really loving and digging who I was awakening unto and it felt great.

Now that loving myself was becoming easier, I began to place my focus also on loving another in an intimate relationship. In my studies of love patterns in relationships, I developed a program called the "Love Rekindled Program" where I created four different "Love Styles". These are the patterns that most women tend to demonstrate love in their relationships. One of love styles is called "The Starver". My love style was to starve a relationship. I would do all of the right things such as clean, cook, etc., but when it came to getting close, not just sexually, but intimately, I would freeze up. I held a false belief that if he gets too close, he will not love me and he will leave me. In my quest to learn new love patterns, I had to release that old false self-defeating belief that I held about myself and recognize that "I was not that woman." Knowing that I was lovable and fully acknowledging that I was worthy of getting to know, shifted my mindset to a belief that not only was love possible for me, it was inevitable.

I never let go of my desire for a loving relationship. I was sitting at my desk one day and I felt this overwhelming urge to write a letter. I felt God wanted me to write a letter to my future husband. So I did. I addressed the letter to "My Divine Right Mate." As I put the pen to the paper, the words just flowed out of me like a water fall. I wasn't thinking, I was just writing what I was hearing and it felt so good. When I finished writing and read it, I felt such love swell within me. It felt right, it felt good, and it was good. I folded the letter and placed it in an envelope, sealed it and wrote on the outside of the envelope, "To My Divine Right Mate." I knew in that moment that it was just a matter of time that I would meet him and the "when it happens" no longer mattered, because I knew it would happen. When we let go of the "how" and the "when", our dreams will manifest. As we are release it to God and the universe, our dreams will arrive at the divine right time. When we let go and release the need to control the outcome, we are making room for unlimited possibilities that we have not even considered. Because God really can dream a dream for us bigger than we can. Then one day it happened, I met my divine right mate. He was everything I had written in my letter. I remember reading the letter to him and he just looked at me as to say... "It is I." I married him within the same year we met and he still is everything I wrote in that handwritten letter.   This is the first time I have ever shared this letter with anyone other than my husband. But I wanted you to read it:

This letter is written to you, my divine right mate, where ever you may be in this world. I'm writing this letter to you even before I've met you, because I know in my heart that you will exhibit the following:

I love you baby because of who you are. You are not afraid to share your true nature with me. You love God above anyone or anything in life. You nourish and protect the relationship you have with God. You love me with that same intensity you did when we first fell in love. You tell me daily how much you love, and don't mind re-assuring, me because you understand that I need your reassurance. You have a real sense of purpose and direction for your life as well as for ours together. You lead our family with strength as well as gentleness. You are consistent, constant and stable. You hold me tight when I need your protection, yet you allow me the freedom to fly my wings.

I know and trust that I can lean on your shoulders and will not fall, yet you are even willing to carry me when my journey gets to tough. I can trust you with my fears and you won't judge me. You allow me to love you intensely and you don't draw back. You listen to me without judgment. You accept my opinions and treat them with respect. You accept my passion with ease. You are my friend, my lover, my partner, my man and even my father when needed. You protect me, you offer me security, and you honor me. I honor you, I respect you and I am willing to follow you, because I can trust your decisions and choices. You allow me in your space, yet you still keep your identify and allow me to keep mine. You are a wonderful father and you love my kids as your own. You will allow me to love your kids (if you have some.) You understand and accept that I can never have any more children, but you love me anyway and that's okay with you.

I can trust you to fix the crisis and always remain in complete control of the situation. You lead, but not rule. You forgive easily and don't hold grudges. You trust me with your deepest, hidden feelings and with your love. You even trust me with your fears. We share our dreams and respect the ones that we are not a part of. When I look into your eyes, they tell me how much you love me. The world can see our love for each other. We respect each other's families and we are not threatened by the relationships we have with them.

You are affectionate and you publicly display that affection towards me. You are sensitive; you send me flowers and gifts, "just because." Holidays are important to you because they mean so much to me. You spend quality time with me and the kids. You make love with your heart, not just your body. You love my body just as it is and you make love to me with passion, gentleness and you communicate what's in your heart during our love making. You allow me to nurture you. You love my cooking, my housekeeping and the way I pamper you. You encourage me, you never yell at me and you never hit me or emotionally abuse me.

You are competent with your finances and with ours together. You invest our money wisely and consider my opinions in money matters. You protect your credit and honor your commitments. You plan for our future and retirement. You never cheat on me and you are always faithful. You accept my flaws and imperfections and I accept yours. Most of all, I love you because you are you and that I know you were divinely sent. You were worth waiting for my darling. I love you, Angela

When reading this letter, you will notice how needy I was at that time. Underneath all of the neediness was that little girl who only wanted to be loved. Once I let go of my neediness and tucked the letter away, God honored my letter by sending me Bill, my divine right mate. Together we share an amazing life with our blended family. He is my divine right mate and is everything that was written in my letter. But he could not show up in my life until I learned to love myself and no longer had need of him. Everything that I needed was already within me; and I do mean everything.

When I met Bill, it was during a time in my life when I was happy and my life was fulfilling. I had become so happy with my life and so fulfilled living with a purpose, that I almost missed Bill when he showed up. He arrived in my life during a time when a relationship was the furthest from my mind. I had found my joy…I had found love within myself. It is when we don't need someone that we are truly ready to love.

For years, I had allowed others to write the script for my life and now know that I have the power to rewrite it as I want it to be. I wanted my own love story and it was within me. Only what I was not giving to myself was missing. I was not giving love to myself; so no one else could. Once I changed, this amazing invisible story began to unfold in my life.

You must be willing to give to yourself that which you want from others. If you want honesty and integrity from others, how honest are you with yourself? If you want someone to be nice and kind to you, how nice and kind are you to yourself? Do you treat yourself well by not putting a lot of sugar in your body and getting proper rest? It is an unkind thing to want someone to do for you what you are unwilling or incapable of doing for yourself.

In rewriting our stories, it is important to understand that we cannot change what has happened in our lives. There is nothing that we could ever do to change the past. But we do have the power to change the beliefs that we hold about what happened to us. For example, my father abandoned me. That is a fact and there is nothing that I can ever do the change that fact. The belief that I held about this fact is that my father's absence caused me to struggle with a low self-image and a lack of self-love. This became my truth and became the underlying source of my behaviors and life experiences. I held an emotion attached to this truth and any time there is an emotion attached to your truth, you have the power change it. As I began to evolve and grow, my truth became elevated to God's Ultimate Truth and God's Ultimate Truth says that I am loved, lovable and powerful beyond measure. When we allow God's Ultimate Truth to super-exceed our limited truth about our stories, a new story can begin to unfold naturally causing our life experiences to be transformed.

God's Ultimate Truth allows us to see the whole, entire truth and not just our limited view of the truth. Once this happens, we no longer have to continue telling the same old stories because our new stories have become our new reality. Many women are stuck in their old stories because they have not allowed the truth they've held about their stories to raise to the level of God's Ultimate Truth.

We can all rewrite our own love story. Perhaps your love story is not a relationship; maybe it's a new career choice. Maybe you want to leave your job and start a business as your love story. Whatever you want in your life, you have the power to revive and rewrite your own love story. It's time to tell a new story, but this time on your own terms and this time based on God's Ultimate Truth. This is your story... and your love story really does begin with you.

Summary:

The seventh step to "My Journey to Being": Rewrite Your Own Love Story

My Defining Moment:

That I could at any moment change my life and that I had the power to rewrite my own love story.

Steps to rewriting your love story:

1. Decide what you want.
2. Recognize that only what you are not giving is missing. Give that which you seek.
3. What truth have you been telling yourself about your story that you can change by replacing it with God's Truth?
4. Revive and rewrite your story now.

Ritual:

Take off all of your clothes and stand in front of a full length mirror. Look at every single part of your imperfect body and see it as perfect. Then lean in closer to look into your eyes. Don't be surprised at the uneasy feeling you experience at first. You will have an intense urge to stop it and not go on with it, but push past the fear. Lean into the mirror and look yourself squarely in the eyes, say to yourself, "_____ I love you." Repeat this process seven times.

9

A Brand New Me and a Brand New Destiny

My life has been filled with stories: stories of shame, stories of pain, stories of guilt and stories of regret. It was when I learned to rewrite my story that my life began to take on a new form. I once heard someone ask, "What would your life be like without that story?" That was such a profound question. But I realized that without that story, I could not have the life I now know. It is because of that story this book has been written. And it is because of that story; I now know that I have the power to rewrite myself a new story. And so do you.

If you are not happy with the way your life is currently, then change it. If the story you are now living isn't what you want, then rewrite it. But this time, on your terms. Stop telling that story, stop remembering that story and start reclaiming your new story. Our lives become filled with many turns and detours, but we get to decide which direction we want to go. We get to decide who we will become and what we will do.

Being made a fatherless daughter through my father's absence and his inability to show me the love I yearned for could no longer determine my destination in life. Being a fatherless daughter does not define who we are. It simply helps to shape and awaken us unto who we were meant to be. We have to step out of who we aren't, step out of our history and reclaim our power to be, our right to be and our right to exist. Leave behind the story that no longer serves you and rewrite the story of your new life.

Every woman, fatherless daughter or not, has the same God-given right to be who she was meant to be. You only need to give yourself permission to do so. Each week, through my work, I have the pleasure of speaking with women from around the world, who feel stuck in their stories of life. They can't seem to find the strength and the courage to stand in their power. Many don't even recognize that they have such power. This is why I do what I do. I want every woman to understand that she can, at any moment, write a new story. Who says the story has to end that way? You get to choose. It's just that no one has ever told you that you could.

As women, we've been conditioned to believe that if we try to step out of the box that has been designed for us; we are either: too selfish, too radical, too independent, or too masculine. We then become afraid. We become fearful of being left alone or fearful of not being loved. But it is when a woman stands in her true authentic power, gets completely clear about who she is and what she wants, that she radiates with a beauty that is undeniably magnetic. There's nothing more beautiful and more powerful than an awakened woman. A woman who is no longer sleepwalking and no longer blinded to the false illusion of who the world says she has to be.

No one has the right to tell you who you can or cannot be. No one has the right to tell you what your life must be. When I understood that I could choose my life, I stood up and declared with a big shout to the world, "I'm Not That Woman!" I am a brand new me and I have a brand new destiny. And life for me has never been the same.

Today, I have a new story. It is one of renewal, forgiveness, transformation, celebration and love. You too can start anew at any moment of your life. Every day, I teach women from around the world the keys that I've shared in this book and I get to witness the remarkable stories that are being discovered as these women learn how to connect deeply with their authentic selves and authentic power. As they remember who they are by removing the false illusions of the mask they wear, they get to move closer to Love.

They have learned how to release what no longer serves them through the amazing power of forgiveness; therefore reactivating their lives by discovering their true purpose. As they recover what they gave away and reclaim their right to exist, they can step into the space of contribution by re-establishing their place in the world. Over and over again, I get the privilege of watching them rewrite their stories and see them live their dreams. They have learned that they don't have to settle for what shows up in their lives. And neither do you. You can choose again. Life gives to all of us an endless supply of new possibilities and new beginnings.

It is my desire that this book has given you the power to recognize what your life can be. Not in some radical sense of the way, but it is through the power of love that we can all transform our lives and the world around us. Love is the cohesive power that holds the universe together. It stands to reason that it can hold all of our chaotic lives together as well. When we learn to love ourselves and others from the depths of our souls we get to experience a remarkable and incredible new journey.

I was a woman without a voice, without hope and without love. I searched for a soft place to lay my heart in the arms and beds of men who didn't love me or want me. I tried to numb the painful feelings of loneliness and despair with shopping and with food. But nothing would take away the pain permanently. It was only by the grace and mercy of a loving and kind God who gently reached out and showed me what real love was, that my heart could finally find a place to call home.

We are all a part of a large invisible story that is unfolding each and every moment of our lives. You and I are the principle players in this story and only we are the only ones who can be cast for the parts. There can be no stand-ins. There can be no understudies or substitutes. We have got to show up for this story. As we show up, the story will unfold in unimaginable ways that goes beyond this mere physical plane. And the results will be filled with love, joy and happiness. But you've got to show up. I'm talking about the real, authentic you. If you insist on projecting your false self all over the place, then you really are not showing up at all. Someone else is living and writing your story for you. Take back your power and reclaim your life. It's your birthright to do so.

You are more than what you see in the mirror. If you would just look a little deeper, you will see a remarkable, beautiful and unique expression of divine love. And as we embrace these larger parts of ourselves, we will expand into new horizons. Your destiny has been and always will be Love. Love is the destination for all of us. On this journey, there will be stops along the way that we can enjoy, some that we may stay over to learn a lesson or two, but we will always head to our real destination in life. And that, my sisters, is love.

On some level we've all been inside that caterpillar who others wanted to call a worm. But like I said before, you knew somewhere deep down that you were a caterpillar waiting to be transformed into a beautiful butterfly. This book has served as your cocoon. And now the butterfly is ready to leave the cocoon. It's time to take your flight!

Happily ever after is not just for the fairy tales, it is for you and I. All of our stories begin with, "Once upon a time…" and they can all end with "lived happily, ever after." You and I get to choose what happens in the middle. Ha, ha! And that makes the journey worthwhile!

10
Take the Vow to Love

For years I went through life never really understanding why no one would see me or love me. I struggled to find true love and real financial success, running from one great idea to another and one man's arms to another. My life seemed like one roller coaster ride after another.

After coming down from one let down after another, I finally reached my desperation point where I'd had enough. I was either going to get it right or just quit altogether. Yes, I contemplated ending it all because I couldn't just keep going. I felt like someone was trapped inside of me wanting to be free, but couldn't.

Then one day, I realized that there *was* someone trapped inside of me. It was the real me. My authentic self wanted to break free from the false illusions of my religious beliefs, cultural beliefs, family beliefs and my own sabotaging limiting beliefs. I wish that I could tell you that my road to freedom was as simple as these seven guiding principles in this little book, but it wasn't.

While I used these principles as a guide to how I live my life daily, it also took the help of my loving mentors, coaches and others to help me on this journey. Your life is not an isolated island whereby you can live it alone. No, you were born as a relational being and you need the help of others to find your way home to love.

This book is not meant to be a cure-all to your life's issues, nor does it promise to make everything right. It will however, provoke you into thinking about the direction in which your life is taking you and hopefully offer you some new perspectives and alternate routes.

Learning to live by these principles can help you to discover answers to many of the questions you may have. They will also help to start a much needed conversation about what you want in life, how you want to live your life, who you want to live it with and what you want to live it doing. It will also get you started to exploring your life from a deeper space, a space where most of us dare not go. It takes courage to go into the deeper spaces of our lives and admit things that we would rather not acknowledge. But it is necessary when we want to find and discover new ways for living.

I believe that we all must arrive at a defining moment in ourselves. A moment where we are willing to move beyond our comfort zones and explore the new horizons that await us, knowing that all miracles can only take place outside of the comfort zone. For years, my comfort zone was me playing the victim of being a fatherless daughter. I had allowed my entire life to be fueled from this one missing link. While it was a huge missing link in my life as a child, I came to realize that I was not a child any longer. I was not a victim any longer. "I was not that woman." I could be a brand new me with a brand new destiny.

I decided that it was time to tell a new story. It was time to rewrite my own love story. My love story began with me; it was choosing me and not someone else. Embracing love as a lifestyle is now my focus and I want to ask you to join with me on this journey.

Let's face it!! Our world is changing and we are faced with many challenges; some that we've never faced before. Our leaders are still fighting, yet they have failed to find solutions that work for all of us. Our enemies have threatened us, yet we've failed at finding ways to create peace and a cease fire. Our financial institutions have failed us with their unrelenting greed, yet we've not discovered ways to break through their powers. Violence seems to be the way we've learned to solve our problems, yet it has only brought us more sorrow and pain.

Only love can conquer hate. Only love will help us to see every human being as God's creation. Only love will cause men and women everywhere to think more deeply about how they show up in life each day. Love will drive us to change how we behave and to value our most priceless treasure...Life Itself.

At the writing of this book, I am in the midst of what I call a global launch. We call it "Take the Vow to Love" movement. What we aim to do at the "Take the Vow" movement is to inspire millions to begin to understand the powerful force of love and learn ways to use it as the power base from which we source our lives. Simply put...learn new ways of being.

We believe as we convince millions from around the world to begin to consciously embrace love as a lifestyle, there will be a critical shift within our midst and we will witness and experience a radical unleashing of a new and brighter world for all of us.

We will be launching our official website, along with several "Take the Vow to Love" online events and face-to-face gatherings in various parts of the world. If you desire to receive updates on our progress, pre-launch event notices and news about the official launch, simply complete the box to the right on the website to get on our official list.

Marianne Williamson said, "We are making one of the largest turn of the hearts, than ever before in human history." This is exactly what we are doing with the "Take the Vow to Love" global movement.

We want to thank you in advance for joining what we recognize as the ending of one era and the emergence of a new and more powerful one. We can no longer be neutral. We must all take a stand and begin to create a better world for us all. Remember, live authentically, laugh every day and embrace love as a lifestyle. Because success in life really does begin with love. www.takethevowtolove.com

ABOUT THE AUTHOR

Angela Carr Patterson is a speaker, author, life strategist coach, corporate trainer and radio talk show host. She is known internationally as The Love Lifestyle Coach; because she help women take love and transmit it to transform their lives and the world around them. She is a Fatherless Daughter Advocate, where she offers support and information to help these women embrace self-love, acceptance and forgiveness. Angela is the mother of five adult children, two granddaughters and she resides in Columbia, SC, with her husband, Bill and their dog, Cody.

For more information: visit www.thelovelifestyle.com

Made in the USA
Charleston, SC
30 May 2013